20108492

ELIZABETH CADY
STANTON
SOCIAL REFORMER

SPECIAL LIVES IN HISTORY THAT BECOME

Signature LIVES

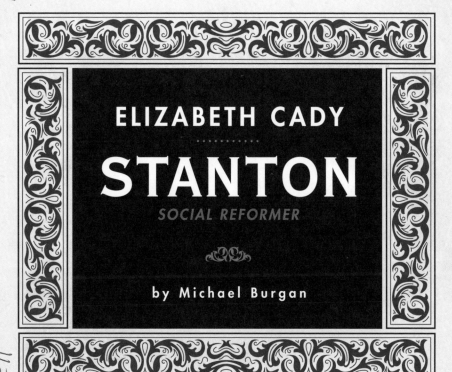

ELIZABETH CADY
STANTON
SOCIAL REFORMER

by Michael Burgan

Content Adviser: Martha Gardner, Ph.D.,
Assistant Professor, Department of History,
DePaul University

Reading Adviser: Rosemary G. Palmer, Ph.D.,
Department of Literacy, College of Education,
Boise State University

COMPASS POINT BOOKS MINNEAPOLIS, MINNESOTA

Compass Point Books
3109 West 50th Street, #115
Minneapolis, MN 55410

Visit Compass Point Books on the Internet at *www.compasspointbooks.com*
or e-mail your request to *custserv@compasspointbooks.com.*

Editor: Jennifer VanVoorst
Lead Designer: Jaime Martens
Photo Researcher: Marcie C. Spence
Page Production: Heather Griffin
Cartographer: XNR Productions, Inc.
Educational Consultant: Diane Smolinski

Managing Editor: Catherine Neitge
Creative Director: Keith Griffin
Editorial Director: Carol Jones

Library of Congress Cataloging-in-Publication Data
Burgan, Michael.
  Elizabeth Cady Stanton: social reformer / by Michael Burgan.
     p. cm. — (Signature lives)
  Includes bibliographical references and index.
  ISBN 0-7565-0990-4 (hard cover)
  1. Stanton, Elizabeth Cady, 1815–1902. 2. Social reformers—United
States—Biography. 3. Suffragists—United States—Biography. I. Title.
II. Series.
  HQ1413.S67B87 2005
  305.42'092—dc22   2005002794

Table of Contents

1 FIGHTING FOR VOTING RIGHTS

Chapter

❦⟨✕⟩❦

On a sunny summer morning, horse-drawn wagons rolled along the dirt roads of Seneca Falls, New York. The passengers inside these wagons—both men and women—were heading to a local church. A few days before, they had read a simple ad in the local newspaper, inviting them to a "Woman's Rights Convention … to discuss the social, civil, and religious rights of women." No one had ever called for a meeting like this before. The 300 or so people who came to the church on July 19, 1848, did not know what to expect.

The church in Seneca Falls was filled with an eager audience as Elizabeth Cady Stanton began to speak. Stanton, one of the five local women who had planned the convention, was well-educated about

Elizabeth Cady Stanton addressed the first women's rights convention in Seneca Falls, New York, in 1848.

law and government. She believed women had a duty to use the political system to claim their legal rights as Americans. Still, Stanton had never spoken in public before on women's issues. Some people in the crowd struggled to hear her voice. But her words carried a strong message. Her words changed history. She read:

We hold these truths to be self-evident: that all men and women are created equal; that they are endowed by their Creator with certain inalienable rights; that among these are life, liberty, and the pursuit of happiness.

In the Declaration of Sentiments, Stanton and the other women asserted that they were entitled to the same rights as men because they were in fact equal to men: "Resolved, That woman is man's equal—was intended to be so by the Creator, and the highest good of the race demands that she should be recognized as such."

The document Stanton read was called the Declaration of Sentiments. In their declaration, Stanton and her friends urged society to give women an equal role and offered a series of 12 resolutions that summed up what they wanted changed. This declaration of the rights of women was based on the Declaration of Independence and formed the centerpiece of the Woman's Rights Convention.

The women's Declaration of

In CONGRESS, July 4, 1776.

The unanimous Declaration of the thirteen united States of America.

Sentiments called for sweeping changes in attitudes and policies toward women. Most important to Stanton, however, was a woman's right to vote. Only if women had suffrage could they elect leaders who

The colonies' Declaration of Independence was the basis for the women's Declaration of Sentiments.

would listen to their concerns. And the women's right to vote sprang from the same idea that gave men that right. In the U.S. political system, "no just government can be formed without the consent of the governed." Since the laws affected women, they had a right to help shape those laws. "The right is ours," Stanton said. "Have it we must. Use it we will."

Not everyone at the convention agreed with Stanton on women's suffrage. Before the meeting, her husband, Henry, had told her not to include suffrage in the declaration. Though he actively supported women's rights, he believed the country was not ready for women's suffrage. Too many Americans still believed women lacked the intelligence to understand politics and vote wisely. The opponents of suffrage said that husbands and fathers represented their wives and daughters when they stepped into the voting booth. Stanton rejected those arguments. Suffrage, she claimed, was the key issue for making women equal in America.

The people attending the convention debated the resolutions added to the end of the Declaration of Sentiments. All the resolutions won the support of almost everyone there—except the resolution on women's suffrage. The audience accepted Stanton's radical idea of women's suffrage by just a few votes.

By calling for a women's rights convention,

Stanton and her friends hoped to challenge the ideas and laws that restricted what women could and could not do. In Stanton's time, American women had few legal rights. When women married, they were expected to obey their husbands. Any property a woman owned before her marriage became her husband's, and husbands controlled any money their wives earned at jobs outside the home. The laws also made it hard for a woman to divorce a man who

In the early 1800s, running a household was the woman's job.

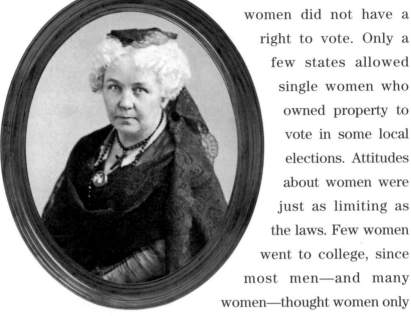

Elizabeth Cady Stanton

treated her badly, and most women did not have a right to vote. Only a few states allowed single women who owned property to vote in some local elections. Attitudes about women were just as limiting as the laws. Few women went to college, since most men—and many women—thought women only needed to know how to raise children and run a household. Women were also not allowed to speak in churches or at social events where men were present.

For years, Stanton had raised a family and done what was expected of a 19th-century woman. But as time went on, she grew tired with simply looking after her children and the servants who helped care for them. As she later wrote, "I suffered with mental hunger, which, like an empty stomach, is very depressing." Stanton also saw that many women around her had even harder lives. Some lacked the money to hire servants, while others lived with husbands who drank too much or refused to help around the home. In 1848, she made a decision: "Some active measures should be taken to remedy the wrongs of society in general, and of women in particular."

For the rest of her life, Elizabeth Cady Stanton would write and speak on equal rights for women. Although suffrage was important to her, it was not her only goal. Stanton wanted new laws that made it easier for women to divorce their husbands. She tried to improve wages and conditions for women who worked outside the home. She also worked on behalf of African-Americans—first as part of the abolitionist cause, and later in pursuit of universal suffrage.

Still, voting rights for women was Stanton's life-long mission. She did not, however, live to see women win the right to vote. She died almost 20 years before the 19th Amendment to the U.S. Constitution granted suffrage to all women. But Stanton is remembered as one of the most forceful founders of the women's movement, the effort to give American women the same legal rights as men. ❧

Chapter
2 A PRIVILEGED YOUTH

❧❧❧

The Seneca Falls church where Elizabeth Cady Stanton made history sat about 150 miles (240 kilometers) west of her hometown of Johnstown, New York. Elizabeth was born in Johnstown on November 12, 1815. Her father, Daniel Cady, was a wealthy lawyer and judge, and the year before Elizabeth was born he was elected to Congress. Margaret Livingston Cady, Elizabeth's mother, was related to the Livingston family that had dominated New York politics and business since colonial days. By all accounts, the Cadys were the "first family" of Johnstown, with their wealth and political connections.

Margaret and Daniel Cady had a large family, with a total of 11 children—six girls and five boys.

In later life, Elizabeth Cady Stanton often called herself a "Daughter of the Revolution." She was referring to the American Revolution, and its aim of winning independence for the United States. Stanton saw herself leading an equally important battle for women's independence from men. Stanton also had a strong family tie to the American Revolution. Her grandfather, Colonel James Livingston (1747–1832), helped catch a British spy. Livingston's heroics ended a plot to give the British the American fort at West Point, New York.

Only one of the boys lived to adulthood, however. Elizabeth was the fourth of the six girls, and one of her earliest memories was the birth of her youngest sister, Catherine. Elizabeth was 4 years old at the time. She later wrote about watching family friends coming to visit the new baby. The friends said over and over, "What a pity it is she's a girl!" As an adult, Elizabeth realized how those feelings reflected the common thinking of the day—that girls were considered an inferior order of beings.

The Cadys lived in a two-story wooden home when Elizabeth was born. They later moved into a much larger brick house, where Mr. Cady ran his law business and trained new lawyers. Inside the Cady home, servants helped Mrs. Cady raise her children and do daily chores. Mrs. Cady was a tall woman who spoke her mind. Elizabeth said her mother was "the soul of independence ... cool in the hour of danger and never knowing fear." Elizabeth would later show the same independence and strength herself when she fought for women's rights.

To Elizabeth, her parents ran a strict household. Margaret Cady dressed her daughters all in red— a color Elizabeth learned to hate—and slapped their fingers if they fiddled with their scratchy collars. The Cady girls were also forbidden from playing at a nearby stream, although they sometimes ignored their parents and played there anyway. Elizabeth and her sisters also broke their parents' rules when they sneaked into a storeroom filled with food, cloth, and other supplies. As an adult, Elizabeth recalled how she and her sisters secretly enjoyed some of the sweet treats they found there.

Margaret Livingston Cady

Not everything that Elizabeth enjoyed was forbidden. She sailed on a raft on a local pond and roamed through the forests of Johnstown. In the basement of the Cady home, she and her sisters played games. During the wintertime, the local children built snow forts, sledded down hills, and climbed an icy pile of logs they called "the Alps." On the Fourth of July, Elizabeth enjoyed the local celebration, which included a parade, food, and fireworks.

As Elizabeth later admitted, her parents were at times kind, indulgent, and considerate. But her parents were also strongly influenced by their religion. The Cadys belonged to the Presbyterian Church. This Protestant faith had developed in England and Scotland during the 16th century. Presbyterians had strong views about right and wrong behavior, and they tried to live by all the rules set out in the Bible. The Cadys wanted their children to be good Presbyterians, and this meant sometimes limiting what they could do. Dancing, for example, was never allowed in the home. Presbyterians looked down on activities that might take people's attention from God or that focused too much on pleasure. As a girl, Elizabeth felt everything she enjoyed was considered a sin and that all she ever heard from adults was "No!"

Elizabeth began her education with a local woman named Maria Yost. For decades, Miss Yost taught the children of Johnstown the basics of reading and writing. From there, Elizabeth entered the Johnstown Academy. Just before she turned 11, a family tragedy influenced the learning Elizabeth would pursue there—or so she claimed later in life.

In 1826, Eleazar Cady, the family's only surviving

son, returned from college with a deadly illness. When Eleazar died, Mr. Cady felt a deep loss. He told Elizabeth, "I wish you were a boy." As Elizabeth later described the scene, she threw her arms around her father's neck and said, "I will try to be all my brother was." To the young girl, that meant doing "manly" things. She would study the courses boys took, such as Latin, Greek, and mathematics. Elizabeth also pledged to learn how to ride a horse, and eventually she could guide her horse over fences 4 feet (1.2 meters) high. At the Johnstown Academy, Elizabeth took classes with boys several years older than she. She worked hard to prove that she was just as smart as they were—

Daniel Cady

if not more so. She also took private lessons in Greek with a local minister. Competing with boys, she earned a prize for her skill with the Greek language.

Few women of Elizabeth's time pursued an education the way she chose to. Parents, ministers, and teachers expected young women to learn only the basics of reading and writing—if that—and then prepare for becoming a mother and wife. Mr. Cady let Elizabeth do more than most girls of the time. Yet even as Elizabeth did well in school, Mr. Cady was still disappointed with her, because she would never be a boy.

Some historians think Elizabeth might have overstated this episode in her young life. She may have simply wanted to make a point for the women who heard her story. She knew they would share her feelings. Most women of the era would have known men who always looked down on them, no matter what they accomplished. And though Elizabeth wanted to prove to her father how strong and successful she could be, Mr. Cady never completely accepted her fight for women's equality.

In 1830, Elizabeth graduated from the Johnstown Academy. She wanted to go to nearby Union College, but at that time no college in the United States accepted young women. And Mr. Cady thought Elizabeth had all the schooling she would ever need. He suggested that she join him when he rode from town to town, hearing cases for his job as a local judge. Another idea, Mr. Cady said, was that Elizabeth learn "how to keep house and make puddings and pies."

For a time, Elizabeth did what her father wanted, but her real desire was to study. Finally, her brother-in-law Edward Bayard stepped in. He had recently married the Cadys' eldest daughter, Tryphena. The Bayards often acted as parents for the other Cady children. Mr. Cady was often away because of his work, and Mrs. Cady became depressed when her youngest child, another son named Eleazar, died as an infant. For a time, she played less of a role in her other children's lives.

Edward Bayard finally convinced Mr. Cady to let Elizabeth go back to school. In January 1831, she arrived at the Troy Female Seminary. At the time, similar schools taught young women about the arts or how to speak French. An ad for the Troy Seminary promised parents that their daughters would study with "superior music teachers" and claimed that the art teachers had "long experience

Troy Female Seminary was located in Troy, New York—about 40 miles (64 km) southeast of Johnstown.

With her husband, John Willard, Emma Hart Willard (1787–1870) founded the Troy Female Seminary in 1821. The school was the first in the United States to offer women an education similar to what men received in colleges. Like Elizabeth Cady Stanton, Emma Hart Willard thought women should be well-educated. She did not, however, want the political equality that Stanton sought. Willard accepted traditional beliefs about the chief roles women should play—wife and mother. In 1895, the Troy Female Seminary was named the Emma Willard School, and it still exists today.

and tried ability." Yet Emma Hart Willard, the head of the Troy Seminary, also offered courses usually taught only to men at colleges and universities. The young women at her school studied such subjects as mathematics, science, politics, history, and philosophy.

During her first year at Troy, Elizabeth was swept up in the excitement of a new religious movement called the Second Great Awakening. The first had taken place during colonial times, starting in the 1740s. In both cases, preachers traveled across the countryside. They spoke at large public meetings called revivals, since the preachers hoped to revive interest in reading the Bible and being good Christians. The preachers appealed to the crowd's emotions, convincing their audiences to admit their sins and accept Jesus Christ into their lives.

Elizabeth often went to hear a preacher named Charles Finney. He was the most famous "revivalist" in upstate New York. Elizabeth described how he spoke with his "great eyes rolling" and "his arms flying about in the air like those of a windmill." Finney's ideas were similar to some of the Presbyterian teachings the Cadys had taught their children. Elizabeth began to spend many hours thinking about how to serve God and avoid going to hell. At times, she went home and woke her father in the middle of the night, begging him to pray for her.

The Cady family began to worry about Elizabeth's new, strong interest in religion. They thought she might damage her health, since she worried so much about her sins and going to heaven. Edward Bayard began to show her books on science and urged her to discuss what she read. Slowly, Elizabeth lost interest in the revivals. As she grew older, Elizabeth rejected the faith she once had. She developed her own ideas, and at times even doubted the existence of God. Later in life, these attitudes made Elizabeth unpopular with many Americans—even women who supported her political beliefs. ℘

PIONEERS · OF ·

CHAS. SUMNER.

HENRY WARD BEECHER.

WENDELL PHILLIPS.

WM. LLOYD GARRISON.

GERRIT SMITH.

HORACE GREELEY.

HENRY WILSON.

FREEDOM.

3 *Chapter*
THE ABOLITIONIST CAUSE

❧❧❧

In 1833, Elizabeth Cady graduated from the Troy Female Seminary and returned to Johnstown. She had mixed feelings about her years at the school. She had always played and studied with boys, and she sometimes missed not being around them. Yet Elizabeth was glad she went to Troy and had a chance to meet Emma Willard. She later called Willard one of the remarkable women of the time.

In her autobiography, she called the period after she left Troy "the most pleasant years of my girl-hood." Although her formal schooling had ended, Elizabeth continued to learn. She and her friends would often discuss ideas with her brother-in-law, Edward Bayard. At times, he read novels to the young women or questioned them about history, politics, and law. Elizabeth also talked with the young men who came to study law with her father. Some of them took an interest in her. She was considered pretty, with her fair skin, dark hair, and blue eyes. At times she found some of the young men she met attractive, but she did not have any serious boyfriends. Her real wish was to dazzle the law students with her intelligence, so they would consider her their equal.

Elizabeth enjoyed spending time with her brother-in-law and her friends. She also looked forward to visiting her cousin Gerrit Smith, who lived in central New York. Smith was one of the wealthiest men in America, thanks to land he owned in several states. But Smith did not show off his wealth. He preferred to use it to help others.

Like Elizabeth, Smith had been affected by the Second Great Awakening. His new interest in Christianity led him to support many reform movements. The Second Great Awakening stirred a similar spirit in many well-educated people in New York. Their faith drove them to try to solve any social or political problems they saw around them. Some of the reformers called for temperance. They believed people who drank too much alcohol harmed others around them. In particular, alcoholic men often could not work and support their families. They could also become violent and abuse their wives and children. Other reformers wanted to improve conditions in prisons and increase the number of public schools. Smith took an interest in many of these issues, but most important to him was abolishing slavery.

Since the end of the American Revolution in 1783, the Northern states had been slowly ending slavery. In the South, however, slavery remained a part of daily life. White plantation owners were convinced their farms would collapse if they did not

Southern plantation owners relied on slaves for labor-intensive tasks such as picking cotton.

Gerrit Smith's home in Peterboro, New York, was one stop on the Underground Railroad. This "railroad" was actually a network of people that helped runaway slaves. Both whites and free blacks served as "conductors" and "stationmasters" on the railroad. They helped escaped slaves reach Canada, where they would gain their freedom. Some people in the Underground Railroad actually traveled with the slaves, guiding them from one safe spot to the next. Others, such as Smith, had barns or secret rooms in their houses where they hid the slaves from police officers or slave owners.

have slaves raising such crops as cotton and tobacco. Slaves also played an important role in Southern cities, holding such jobs as ship maker, carpenter, and blacksmith. Abolitionists such as Smith and his friends wanted to end slavery immediately across the United States. During the 1830s and 1840s, however, few Americans, even in the North, shared their views. Southerners believed they had a legal right to own slaves, since the U.S. Constitution did not forbid it. Many Northerners were racists and did not want freed black slaves leaving the South and settling in their states.

Elizabeth had grown up around African-Americans. Her family hired three black servants. One of them, Peter, often took the Cady daughters around town. Peter loved Elizabeth and her sisters deeply, and they returned the feeling. At times, the girls went with him to his church. Peter was the only African-American in the church, and he had to sit by himself. But Elizabeth and her sisters sat with Peter, instead of sitting with the other white people. From a young age, Elizabeth saw that some people judged others by the color of their skin, and she realized it was wrong.

With her cousin Gerrit and his friends, Elizabeth heard discussions about personal rights and freedom. She also learned about the abolitionist movement. She met slaves for the first time, since they sometimes stayed at the Smith house after running away from their masters. One of the runaways she met was a teenage girl. Elizabeth later wrote:

> *For two hours we listened to the sad story of her childhood and youth, separated from all her family and sold ... in a New Orleans market when but fourteen years of age. ... We all wept as she talked, and ... needed no further education to make us earnest abolitionists.*

In 1839, while staying with her cousin, Elizabeth met an abolitionist named Henry Stanton. She heard him speak in public against slavery and was impressed with how "he could make his audience both laugh and cry." Ten years older than Elizabeth, Stanton was a good-looking, intelligent man who shared her interest in reform. Only a few weeks after he met Elizabeth, Henry Stanton asked her to marry him. She gladly accepted.

Gerrit Smith, however, saw a problem with the match. He knew Elizabeth's father. Judge Cady was a conservative man. Calling for an immediate end to slavery was a radical notion at the time, and Cady would not like to hear that his daughter was marrying an abolitionist. Tryphena and Edward Bayard also questioned the match.

Inspired by preacher Charles Finney, Henry Stanton studied for the ministry at Lane Theological Seminary in Cincinnati, Ohio. The school soon became a center for abolition, with Stanton and his friend Theodore Weld leading the movement there. In 1834, they were part of a group that convinced nearby Oberlin College to accept women, making it the first coeducational college in the United States. The next year, Oberlin accepted African-Americans as well.

Under this assault from her family, Elizabeth called off the wedding. Henry Stanton, however, refused to give up, and Elizabeth still wanted to be with him.

Through the spring of 1840, Henry made plans to attend an anti-slavery convention in London. The trip overseas would last eight months. Elizabeth decided she and Henry should marry before he left, and then she would go with him. As Henry wrote to a friend, Elizabeth feared "to be left behind in the hands of her opposing friends and wishes to go with me that the storm may blow over while she is absent." So on May 1, 1840, the

In his later years, Henry Stanton would move away from abolitionist work, although he always believed in the cause.

couple wed in Johnstown, with just a few friends attending the ceremony. Elizabeth stunned the minister when she insisted she would not use the word *obey* in her wedding vows. Most women of the

The reform movements of the 1830s and 1840s did not end with politics. An abolitionist named Sylvester Graham (1795–1851) called on people to improve their diets as well. He said people should eat plenty of vegetables and bran, avoid meat, alcohol, and caffeine, and exercise often. Graham invented the Graham cracker and helped found the first group for American vegetarians. The Stantons, as well as their friends the Welds and Sarah Grimké, followed Graham's ideas on how to eat.

time accepted the idea that they would have to do what their husbands ordered, and in their wedding vows, wives promised obedience. Elizabeth made no such promise. She believed that she was entering her marriage as her husband's equal.

After the wedding, the Stantons briefly visited Gerrit Smith and then headed to New Jersey to see Henry's friend Theodore Weld. Weld's wife, Angelina Grimké, was also active in the anti-slavery cause, as was her sister Sarah. In 1838, Angelina Grimké had become the first woman to speak to American lawmakers on a political issue, when she appeared before the Massachusetts State Legislature. She asserted a citizen's right to petition the lawmakers about slavery. Henry was one of several abolitionists who had asked her to speak. Elizabeth quickly discovered that she shared many interests with the Welds and Sarah Grimké.

In May, the Stantons sailed for England. On the voyage across the Atlantic Ocean, Elizabeth read books about abolition. She talked about it with her husband and another abolitionist on board, James G. Birney. He had just agreed to run for president of the United States that year as an anti-slavery candidate. By early June, the Stantons were in London, sharing a hotel with other delegates to the convention. These included several American women from female anti-slavery groups.

The presence of the female delegates created problems at the convention. The men who ran the World's Anti-Slavery Convention held a view common at the time: They did not think women should speak in public on political issues or play a major role in the abolitionist movement. Some of the male abolitionists also feared that they would lose support if they backed equal rights for women. They knew most Americans did not think women deserved the same political and legal rights as men. At the convention, a few men did defend the women. American abolitionists Wendell Phillips and William Lloyd

The most famous of the early U.S. abolitionists was William Lloyd Garrison (1805–1879). He published an anti-slavery newspaper called The Liberator, *and in 1833 he founded the American Anti-Slavery Society. He also believed African-Americans had the same legal and political rights as whites, and he was one of the first men to strongly support the women's rights movement. His position caused a split among abolitionists. The ones who did not support women's rights founded their own anti-slavery groups.*

Abolitionist Thomas Clarkson addressed the Anti-Slavery Society in London in 1840.

Garrison said the women delegates had a right to take part in the convention. But most of the men voted against seating the women with the male delegates. The women were forced to sit off to the side, behind a curtain. In protest, Garrison joined them, rather than take part in the debates held during the convention.

Elizabeth Cady Stanton was just a visitor at the convention, not a delegate. But she listened angrily as male delegates argued for keeping the women separate. She later wrote:

> *It was really pitiful to hear narrow-minded bigots ... so cruelly [placing] their own mothers, with the rest of womankind, to absolute [control under] the ordinary masculine type of humanity.*

As the convention ended, Stanton said that the women there shared a common idea: "It is about time some demand was made for new liberties for women." Stanton had no idea then that she would lead that demand. ℘

4 *Chapter*

THE ROAD TO SENECA FALLS

❦

Stanton's trip to London introduced her to new ideas and people. The most important person she met on her trip was Lucretia Coffin Mott, one of the delegates the men refused to accept. Mott was 22 years older than Stanton, but the difference in age did not keep the women from quickly becoming good friends. Mott was a Quaker, a member of a religion called the Society of Friends. Quakers played important roles in the fight to end slavery and win rights for women. According to the Quakers, everyone had the same ability to understand God and feel God's presence. That religious equality meant all people shared the same legal and political rights as well. Women's rights, Mott once wrote, "was the most important question of my life from a very early day."

Before her work with the 1848 Women's Rights Convention, Lucretia Mott (1793–1880) helped organize the Anti-Slavery Convention of American Women in 1837.

While in London, the two women were almost always together. Mott and Stanton visited schools and prisons, toured the city and its sites, and often ate together. Stanton went with Mott when she preached in a London church. It marked the first time Stanton had heard a woman speak in public. Stanton loved listening to Mott talk about both her faith and women's rights. Stanton later wrote that Mott opened her mind to a new world of thought. Before leaving London, the two new friends made a promise. As soon as they could, they would start a group that would fight for women's rights.

The Stantons remained in Europe the rest of 1840, with Henry speaking about abolition. When meeting people, Elizabeth was always ready to laugh and have a good time. She began to think that she was being too lighthearted while her husband was dealing with such an important subject. She told her cousin Gerrit Smith that Henry wished she could be more serious. But to some of the people she met, Elizabeth's easygoing way was one of her charms. Others respected her growing support of women's rights.

When they returned to New York, the Stantons moved in with Elizabeth's family in Johnstown. Henry decided to become a lawyer, and he studied with Mr. Cady. Elizabeth did her own studying as well. She continued to read about politics and law, and she wrote letters to many of the women she had met in London, including Lucretia Mott. Elizabeth also remained active in reform issues, such as temperance and abolition. She agreed with Henry that slavery had to be fought with laws and political action. The couple disagreed, however, on the issue of women's rights. Henry thought reformers should focus on abolition, instead of trying to win equal rights for women.

In March 1842, the Stantons welcomed the first of seven children: a son named Daniel, nicknamed Neil. Elizabeth began to read whatever she could find about motherhood. She soon learned, however, that not much had been written on the subject. And she didn't agree with a lot of what she read or heard from local doctors. When the newborn Neil had a bent collarbone, Elizabeth removed the doctor's wrapping and came up with her own. Her solution worked better than the doctor's. She later wrote of the experience,

One of the thinkers who influenced both Lucretia Mott and Elizabeth Cady Stanton was Mary Wollstonecraft (1759–1851). The two women discussed her ideas soon after they met in London. In 1792, Wollstonecraft wrote a book called A Vindication of the Rights of Women. The book is sometimes called the first major work of the modern women's movement. Wollstonecraft believed women should receive the same education as men and have an equal chance to pursue their interests. Her daughter, Mary Shelley, wrote the classic book, Frankenstein.

Elizabeth Cady Stanton served as her children's doctor more than once. She gave them medicines based on her study of home-opathy. This form of medical care was developed in the early 19th century by a German doctor, Samuel Hahnemann (1755–1843). He used tiny amounts of herbs and minerals to treat illness. In large amounts, these herbs and minerals caused sickness. But in small doses, Hahnemann believed, they helped the body fight off the diseases.

"I learned another lesson in self-reliance. I trusted neither men nor books absolutely after this."

A few months after Neil was born, the Stantons moved to Boston. Henry had found a job there as a lawyer. For the next five years, Elizabeth split her time between Boston and Albany, where the Cadys had a second home. During this time, Elizabeth gave birth to two more sons, Henry and Gerrit. While in Albany, Elizabeth used her spare time to work for a state law that would give married women legal control over their property. She talked to several legislators on the subject, and the law was finally passed in 1848. In Boston, she continued her studies. She also kept in touch with Lucretia Mott, but their plans for a women's group were delayed. For a time, Mott was sick, and she also had problems to address within the Society of Friends. These concerns prevented her from working closely with Stanton.

In 1847, the Stantons moved from Boston to Seneca Falls, New York, where Tryphena and

Edward Bayard now lived. As she settled in to her new home, Elizabeth felt her life lacked something. She missed the buzz of activity she had found in Boston. And being a housekeeper was becoming boring. At first, she took pride in her ability to run a house and raise her children. Henry traveled often for his abolitionist work, and she was the sole parent. Over time, however, Elizabeth needed a change. As she wrote in her autobiography, "Much that was once attractive in [home] life was now

Stanton, shown here with one of her sons, worked tirelessly for women's rights, despite her many duties at home.

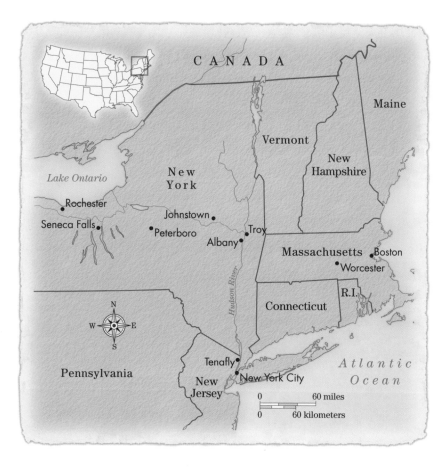

Stanton spent most of her life in New York state.

irksome … my duties were too numerous and varied."

In the summer of 1848, Lucretia Mott came to central New York to visit her friend Mary Ann McClintock. She invited Stanton to join her at the friend's house. McClintock and two other women were also there: Martha C. Wright (Mott's sister) and Jane C. Hunt. All the women were abolitionists and, except for Stanton, all were Quakers. Sitting at a wooden table, Stanton poured out her feelings to the women. She talked about her growing frustration with her life and the general treatment of women. Of the five, Stanton believed most strongly in using politics to improve women's lives. Suffrage, to her, was the key issue for women. Her words, she later wrote, "stirred myself, and the rest of the party, to do and dare anything."

That night, the five women wrote an ad announcing a women's convention. The ad appeared in the Seneca newspaper the next day—July 14, 1848. The convention would meet on July 19 and 20, and on the first day only women would be allowed to attend. A few days later, the women met to write the public statement they would offer for discussion. At first, Stanton wrote, "they felt as helpless and hopeless as if they had been suddenly asked to construct a steam engine." Finally, they decided to copy the form Thomas Jefferson had used in 1776 when he wrote the Declaration of Independence. In the Declaration of Independence, America listed its complaints against King George III of Great Britain. With help from the others, Stanton did the same thing, writing, "The history of mankind is a history of repeated injuries … on the part of man toward woman." This document, which they called the Declaration of Sentiments, then ended with a series of 12 resolutions, summing up what the women wanted changed.

One early male supporter of the women's movement was Frederick Douglass (1818–1895). He and Elizabeth Cady Stanton first met when she lived in Boston. They later spent time together at Gerrit Smith's home. A former slave, Douglass was an abolitionist and journalist. His 1845 autobiography made him famous in Europe—and hated by Southern slave owners. Douglass attended the Seneca Falls convention and defended the idea of giving women the right to vote. Today, he is the best known of the men who signed the Declaration of Sentiments.

Lucretia Mott told Stanton not to expect much of a crowd at the first women's convention. The local farmers and their families would be busy in the fields. Still, about 100 people showed up on the 19th. Some men came, perhaps not realizing only women were invited the first day. Stanton and her friends decided to let the men stay. They and the women heard Stanton call for equal rights for women. The next day, the audience debated the resolutions proposed by Stanton and the others. Finally, 68 women and 32 men signed their names to the Declaration of Sentiments and the resolutions.

Stanton, Mott, and their friends knew they had taken a historic step for women. They hoped more people would support their movement. Instead, Stanton was crushed to see her work ridiculed by the press. One Philadelphia newspaper made fun of the idea that women could do anything important without men. "A woman is nobody," the newspaper read. "A wife

Wesleyan Chapel was the site of the first women's rights convention.

is everything." A New York newspaper attacked the idea of women's suffrage: "We do not see by what principle of right the angelic creatures should claim to compete."

Throughout the rest of the year, Stanton defended the goals of the women's movement in speeches and articles. The Seneca Falls convention also inspired women in other states to organize conventions. The gathering in the New York church had sparked a new movement for women's rights. ✍

5 RIGHTS FOR ALL

ɔ⌇ɔ

In 1849, Elizabeth Cady Stanton began writing articles for a local monthly magazine called *The Lily*. Its publisher was Amelia Bloomer, who favored temperance. At first Stanton did not sign her own name to her articles. Instead, she often called herself "Sunflower." Later, however, she began to sign her initials, E.C.S. She had decided to use both her family name and her husband's name several years before—another sign of her independence as a woman. She did not want to be known simply as Henry Stanton's wife.

For *The Lily*, Stanton wrote about both temperance and women's issues. She called for new laws that made it easier for wives of alcoholics to divorce their husbands. And in one article, she described her

Leaders of the women's movement included (clockwise from top) Lucretia Mott, Elizabeth Cady Stanton, Anna E. Dickinson, Mary Ashton Rice Livermore, Susan B. Anthony, Lydia Marie Francis Child, and Grace Greenwood (center).

dislike for sewing. Women, she wrote, were "slaves to the needle." They wasted their time sewing fancy clothes for themselves because men expected them to dress a certain way. Women also had to sew clothes for their husbands, brothers, and sons. Boys should be taught to sew, Stanton wrote, so they could make their own clothes, and women should do "as little of it as possible."

The first national women's convention was held in 1850 in Worcester, Massachusetts. Stanton was pregnant with her fourth child, Theodore, so she did not attend. Instead, she sent a letter offering ideas on how to run the meeting. For the next decade, Stanton would miss all the national conventions held for women's rights. She had three more children during that time. But she continued to share her ideas with the women who planned the conventions. And with the help of a new friend, she would find other ways to stay active in the women's movement.

In May 1851, Stanton attended an abolitionist meeting in Seneca Falls. On her way home, she saw

Amelia Bloomer standing with another young woman. The new woman smiled as she met Stanton. Her name was Susan B. Anthony. Years later, as she recalled the meeting, Stanton wrote, "I liked her thoroughly." The women talked only briefly that day on the street. But soon they began a friendship that lasted 50 years. Stanton would later write, "In thought and sympathy, we were one."

Anthony knew all about Stanton and her work for women's rights. Her parents had attended a women's convention in Rochester, New York, that Stanton had helped organize. Anthony's major concern was alcohol, and she felt that men in the temperance movement were

denying women a chance to play a meaningful role. She wanted to start a women's temperance movement in New York, and in 1852 she asked Stanton to help. Stanton was soon elected president of the newly created Women's New York State Temperance Society, with Anthony serving as secretary. For Stanton,

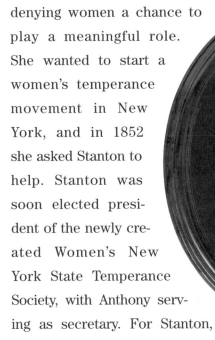

Susan B. Anthony

the temperance movement was a way to address women's rights. She believed women had to play an active role in the fight against alcoholism. Through that action, they could then begin to win their political rights. Over time, Anthony also saw the value of linking major reform efforts, and she joined the fight for women's suffrage.

Stanton and Anthony had different strengths. Stanton was a better writer and speaker, and she wrote many speeches for Anthony. Anthony had the time and energy to organize and attend meetings. When working together on a document, Stanton wrote, Anthony "supplied the facts and statistics," while she supplied the basic ideas and emotions. "Together, we have made arguments that have stood unshaken through the storms of long years," she wrote. And together, Stanton and Anthony formed one of the most important political partnerships ever in U.S. history.

Throughout the 1850s and early 1860s, Stanton

remained close to her home in Seneca Falls. She attended local meetings for temperance, abolition, and women's rights. She continued to write articles and letters to other reformers. She also once again struggled to balance her outside interests and her duties as a mother. Her fifth child, Margaret, was born in October 1852. Stanton showed her physical toughness, walking three miles (4.8 kilometers) to visit friends the day before the child was born.

The Stanton family lived in this house on Washington Street in Seneca Falls, New York.

The day after, Stanton wrote, she "walked … took a ride of three miles … rested an hour or so and then read the newspapers and wrote a long letter."

Stanton still relied on servants to help her raise the children. Henry's law practice and political activities kept him busy, and he was often away 10 months out of the year. Stanton tried to keep the house clean, get the children ready for school, and still find time for herself. She wrote to Anthony in 1853, "How much I long to be free of housekeeping and children, so as to have time to think and read and write."

The next year, Stanton helped organized a women's rights convention in Albany. With Anthony's help, she also prepared a speech that she gave at the convention and later to the New York State Legislature. In it, Stanton described the unfair treatment of women. Unmarried women who owned property had to pay taxes, but they could not elect the lawmakers who decided how much they had to pay. Accused criminals were supposed to face a jury of their peers when they went to court. But since women could not serve on juries, a woman charged with a crime always faced an all-male jury.

On February 14, 1854, Stanton stood before the New York State Legislature. Addressing the assembly of men, Stanton said:

We ask for all that you have asked for yourselves in the progress of your development, since the May Flower cast anchor at Plymouth rock; and simply on the grounds that the rights of every human being are the same and identical.

When the lawmakers heard the speech, they made fun of Stanton for suggesting women should receive equal treatment.

For the next several years, Stanton remained active in the women's movement by writing speeches and attending whatever meetings she could. Her family, however, did not always approve of her work. Even her husband preferred that she not write about women's rights. But as Stanton wrote to Anthony, "I will both write and speak." She just wished she had the same freedom that Anthony had to travel.

Despite her family duties, Stanton continued to work for women's rights, often writing articles for The Lily.

As a mother, Stanton continued to raise her children as she thought best. She did not believe in punishing her children. She preferred using reason to convince them to do what she wanted. She did not force them to go to church, as her parents had done with her and her sisters. Stanton enjoyed playing games with her children and their friends. And she thought children should be allowed to try new things. Adults, she wrote a friend, should boost the confidence of children "and show them how to do what they desire."

Stanton's second daughter Harriot, shown here with her mother in 1856, would later work for women's suffrage as well.

Henry Stanton took an active interest in his children, even though he was often away from home. His political attitudes had changed since he had met Elizabeth. Henry no longer spoke out so often against slavery, although he remained a strong abolitionist. Henry did not want to offend government officials who might be able to give him work. But by 1855, he realized that slavery was the greatest evil in the country. That year, he joined the new Republican Party. Ending the spread of slavery in the United States was one of the party's main goals.

In 1860, Elizabeth Cady Stanton finally began taking a more active role in reform movements. The year before, her father had died. Stanton then began to visit her mother more often. Margaret Cady now frequently baby-sat the Stanton children, giving Elizabeth the freedom to travel. She spoke to women's groups and anti-slavery societies. In one 1860 speech, she said women and African-American slaves were both oppressed by white men:

> To you, white man, the world throws wide
> her gates; the way is clear to wealth, to
> fame, to glory … but the black man and
> the woman are born to shame.

Stanton was thrilled when Abraham Lincoln, a Republican, won the 1860 presidential election. Southerners had talked about seceding, or taking

The Republican Party was founded in 1854. Its first members had belonged to several other parties, including the Free Soil Party, which had actively opposed slavery. The members of the new Republican Party united against the Democrats, who generally were willing to let slavery spread to new U.S. territories and states. In 1856, John C. Frémont ran as the Republican Party's first presidential candidate. Frémont lost, but more Northerners began to support the Republicans.

their states out of the Union, if Lincoln won. The Southerners believed the Republicans would try to end slavery everywhere in the United States. To Stanton and other abolitionists, Southern secession was a good thing. It would mean the United States no longer had slavery within its borders. At the same time, though, Stanton continued to call for the complete abolition of slavery, in case the South did not secede. During several speeches in New York, large mobs came to taunt her and other abolitionists. By "laughing, groaning, clapping, and cheering," Stanton later wrote, the mobs "effectively interrupted the proceedings."

As they had threatened, the Southern states began to secede in December 1860. By the following April, six slave states from the South had formed a new country—the Confederate States of America. Five more states would later join the confederacy. President Lincoln said these states had no legal right to secede. He was ready to go to war to keep them in the Union.

On April 12, 1861, the Civil War began. Stanton and the women she knew were ready to help their country—and fight for the end of slavery. ✍

Jefferson Davis (fourth from left), shown here with his cabinet, was president of the Confederate States of America.

BUILT FROM THE RUINS.

6 CIVIL WAR AND SUFFRAGE

❧❦❧

Elizabeth Cady Stanton believed the Civil War could end slavery, so she strongly supported the North and its war efforts. Stanton hoped that the war would boost support for women's rights. Northern women would do whatever they could to help win the war. Men in the government then might be more willing to give women what they wanted. Susan B. Anthony rejected this notion. She opposed all wars, and she thought this war would ruin the women's movement. Anthony feared that the war would cause people to lose focus on women's rights. Even though they had different ideas, Anthony and Stanton continued to work together. They both fought for abolition as the war went on.

As a loyal Republican, Henry Stanton was

This banner was flown at the 1861 Secession Convention, held in Charleston, South Carolina.

When Lincoln's Emancipation Proclamation took effect on January 1, 1863, it made all slaves in the Confederate states free and gave them the protection of Union troops in the South. The new policy also let African-Americans join the military and fight for the North. This gave the Union new troops at a time when it had trouble finding enough soldiers.

rewarded with a job in the government. This required moving to New York City, and in the spring of 1862 Elizabeth and her family settled into a new home. Elizabeth was glad to return to the excitement of a large city, and she soon began to play an active role in the abolitionist movement there. After January 1, 1863, slavery was no longer allowed in the Southern states. But in the border states, slavery was still legal. These were states that allowed slavery but remained in the Union. Stanton and other female abolitionists demanded the complete abolition of slavery throughout the United States.

In May 1863, Stanton and Anthony founded the Women's Loyal National League. Women who joined promised their loyalty to the Union government—as long as the Civil War was a "war for freedom." The members pledged to collect signatures on petitions and give them to the U.S. Congress. They wanted the national lawmakers to end slavery everywhere and protect the legal rights of the newly freed slaves. Within a year, the league had collected

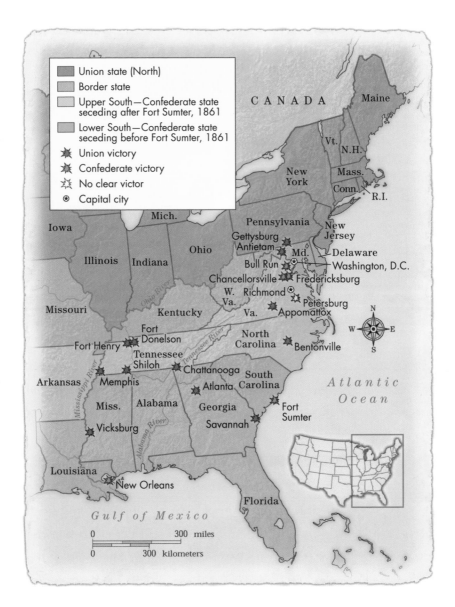

Legend:
- Union state (North)
- Border state
- Upper South—Confederate state seceding after Fort Sumter, 1861
- Lower South—Confederate state seceding before Fort Sumter, 1861
- Union victory
- Confederate victory
- No clear victor
- Capital city

CANADA

Maine

Vt.
N.H.
New York
Mass.
Conn.
R.I.

Mich.
Iowa
Pennsylvania
New Jersey
Ohio
Gettysburg
Antietam
Md.
Delaware
Illinois
Indiana
Bull Run
Washington, D.C.
Chancellorsville
Fredericksburg
W. Richmond
Va.
Va.
Petersburg
Missouri
Kentucky
Appomattox
Fort Donelson
Fort Henry
North Carolina
Bentonville
Tennessee
Shiloh
Chattanooga
Arkansas
Memphis
Atlanta
South Carolina
Atlantic Ocean
Miss.
Alabama
Georgia
Fort Sumter
Vicksburg
Savannah
Louisiana
New Orleans
Florida

Gulf of Mexico

Ohio River
Tennessee River
Mississippi River
Alabama River

| 0 | 300 miles |
| 0 | 300 kilometers |

100,000 signatures.

As 1863 ended, Stanton turned some of her attention to family problems. Henry and the oldest

Civil War battles were fought throughout the South and in the border states.

Stanton son, Neil, both worked at a U.S. customs house. Henry was supposed to stop shippers from smuggling goods into the country. The shippers had to pay a fee that promised their goods were legal. If the shippers lied and the goods were smuggled, they lost the fee. Neil Stanton was accused of stealing some of the fees, and his father soon faced rumors that he had helped his son steal. Neil lost his job right away, and in December Henry was forced to quit. Henry went almost a full year before finding another job, as a newspaper reporter. The episode embarrassed the Stanton family. Elizabeth wrote to a friend that the experience caused her the deepest sorrow of her life.

Going into 1864, Stanton and the Women's League focused on the upcoming presidential election. Stanton and Anthony now both opposed President Lincoln. They thought he was not working hard enough to end slavery and defend the rights of African-Americans. The two women hoped John C. Frémont would be the Republican candidate in the fall. Lincoln still hoped to win the support of the Women's League. He invited the Stantons to the White House. Afterward, Elizabeth said the president was a stronger and better man than she had thought before. Still, she did not favor his reelection.

Most abolitionists, however, supported Lincoln.

John C. Frémont (at left) was Stanton's choice for president in the 1864 election, but he withdrew from the contest because of minimal support.

and he won the election. He also supported the 13th Amendment, which abolished slavery in the United States. Congress approved the amendment in January 1865, and the states ratified it later that year.

On April 9, 1865, the main Confederate army surrendered, ending the Civil War. Just a few days later, the country was stunned by the killing of Abraham Lincoln. As the North and the South made plans to

Confederate General Robert E. Lee (at right) surrendered to Union General Ulysses S. Grant in 1865, ending the Civil War and beginning the period known as Reconstruction.

reunite, no one knew what would happen next. The nation was entering a period called Reconstruction. The United States had to reconstruct, or rebuild, the defeated South. The country also had to reconstruct its laws to accommodate several million newly freed African-American slaves. The job of Reconstruction seemed even more difficult with Lincoln gone. The new president, Andrew Johnson, had once owned slaves himself. In general, he was more conservative than the great president he replaced. At times, he resisted efforts to help African-Americans who had just left slavery.

With slavery ended, abolitionists such as Elizabeth Cady Stanton turned their attention to helping African-Americans win their political rights. Leaders of the women's movement hoped they could also win suffrage for themselves at the same time. In 1865, Congress began to debate the 14th Amendment. It would grant U.S. citizenship to free blacks. Although it did not say so directly, the amendment was also supposed to protect the African-Americans' right to vote. But something in the proposed amendment caught Stanton's eye—and stirred her anger. The rights protected in the amendment only applied to male citizens. For the first time ever, the Constitution would specifically grant legal rights only to

The U.S. Constitution can be amended in two ways. In the first method, two-thirds of the states call for a convention, similar to the one that first created the Constitution in 1787. Any amendments suggested at the convention must then be ratified by three-quarters of the states. In the other method, a member of the U.S. Congress proposes an amendment, and two-thirds of the lawmakers in both the House and Senate must then approve it. Then the amendment goes to the states to be ratified. This amendment method is the only one that has been used.

men. "If that word 'male' be inserted, as now proposed," Stanton wrote, "it will take us a century to get it out again." Stanton knew that only another constitutional amendment would give women their rights, if the 14th Amendment applied just to men.

Stanton and Anthony tried to convince Republican lawmakers to remove the word *male* from the amendment. They collected signatures on petitions, but the lawmakers they talked to refused to present the petitions to Congress. In her anger, Stanton lashed out at African-American males. She had always had good relations with the blacks she knew personally, especially abolitionist Frederick Douglass. She had spent much of her life working to end slavery. But now Stanton claimed that educated white women—such as herself—would make better voters than the newly freed black slaves. She attacked them for their poverty and their ignorance. Stanton's racism surprised and offended some of her old friends. Yet she remained close to some African-

Frederick Douglass

Americans, such as Douglass and Sojourner Truth. Like Douglass, Sojourner Truth was a former slave who became an abolitionist. Truth also joined Stanton in the battle for women's rights.

In May 1866, Stanton and Anthony helped form the American Equal Rights Association (AERA). Its goal was universal suffrage, or voting rights for all, including black

Sojourner Truth

men and white and black women. Later that year, Stanton announced that she wanted to represent part of New York state in Congress. She said that the state constitution forbade women from voting, but it did not stop them from becoming candidates. Stanton ran as an independent, since both the Republicans and Democrats had policies she did not like. She wrote that if blacks received suffrage, "on no principle of justice or safety can the women of the nation be ignored." Not surprisingly, Stanton lost the race. She received only 24 votes.

The next year, Stanton focused her attention on two state conventions. New York held a convention

> Frederick Douglass supported women's suffrage, but he believed that if black suffrage and women's suffrage were to be won separately, black suffrage should come first. "When women because they are women are dragged from their homes and hung upon lampposts ... then they will have the urgency to obtain the ballot," he said.

to amend its state constitution. Stanton hoped to convince delegates to accept universal suffrage. The committee that considered suffrage, however, only called for universal male suffrage. Giving women the vote, a committee report said, was too radical and revolutionary.

Kansas was the other hotspot for universal suffrage in 1867. State voters—all male—were going to vote on whether to give suffrage to African-Americans and women. Male abolitionists in the state wanted to focus on winning the vote for black males. They largely ignored women's suffrage. In September, Stanton and Anthony arrived in the state to work for universal suffrage.

The trip to Kansas was sometimes difficult for Stanton. She was used to living in large, comfortable homes and speaking in churches and halls. She later wrote that on the Kansas prairie, she spoke in log cabins, unfinished schoolhouses, hotels, barns, and in the open air. She and her companions traveled in horse-drawn carriages, since parts of the state lacked railroads. At times, they rolled along dusty paths, not real roads, with no signs to guide them on their journey. They sometimes traveled at night, and Stanton worried her carriage might flip over, sending her into a river. Stanton often slept in the homes of people she met on the road. One night, however, she slept in the carriage, only to be shaken awake by flea-infested hogs that were scratching themselves on the carriage's iron steps.

In the end, voters rejected suffrage for both blacks and women. Still, Stanton thought something good came out of her trip. She wrote to her cousin Libby Smith Miller, "It gave me added self-respect to know that I could endure such hardship … with a great deal of cheerfulness."

After the defeat in Kansas, Stanton and Anthony returned east. With the help of George Francis Train, a millionaire they had met in Kansas, they began publishing a newspaper in 1868. Its name suggested what the women wanted to achieve. They called the newspaper *The Revolution.* ৶

7 THE FIGHT GOES ON

৵ঔ×৯৩

With *The Revolution*, Stanton had a simple goal: "Men, their rights and nothing more: Women, their rights and nothing less." For the next two years, Stanton helped edit the newspaper and wrote many articles for it. She expressed her views on a number of topics, not just on women's suffrage. She and Anthony both believed women should work to resolve many problems affecting the country.

At the time, some factory workers and skilled craftsmen in the United States wanted the right to form labor unions. These groups tried to win better wages and working conditions for their members. Sometimes union members went on strike. By refusing to work, they hoped factory owners would accept their demands. Many businessmen opposed

Elizabeth Cady Stanton claimed her views became more radical as she got older.

strikes and labor unions, as did many politicians. Union leaders often held radical political ideas, such as limiting the right to own private property. Susan B. Anthony had already been working with some labor unions, and she helped educate Stanton on their issues. Stanton came to support the workers' right to strike and to form unions. She also said women should receive equal pay for doing the same work as men.

In *The Revolution,* Stanton used stronger language than ever before to attack men. In one article, she wrote that "the male element is a destructive force ... loving war, violence, conquest." Only women, she said, could limit the harmful habits of men. And the only way they could do that was with the vote. She also wrote articles opposing the 15th Amendment to the Constitution. This amendment made clear that black males had the right to vote. Stanton refused to support the amendment because once again women's suffrage was ignored.

Both men and women who once worked with Stanton now turned against her. To the women, she was taking on too many other issues and losing the focus on suffrage. Stanton was also making too many radical statements. Her views offended men who might have otherwise supported universal suffrage. To male abolitionists, Stanton was an enemy for opposing black suffrage unless women

Stanton used The Revoltion to share her views on women's rights.

also received the right to vote. The abolitionists thought black male suffrage should come first.

In May 1869, Stanton attended a meeting of the American Equal Rights Association. The nasty feelings that some members had for her quickly bubbled to the surface. As a result, Stanton made plans to

Soon after it formed, the NWSA made a legal argument for women's suffrage. Stanton and others claimed that the Constitution already gave women the right to vote. Women were citizens, and no state could take away a citizen's rights, which included suffrage. A Missouri woman named Virginia Minor tested this claim in 1872. She filed a legal suit when she was denied a chance to vote. Eventually, the U.S. Supreme Court ruled that women did not already have a constitutional right to vote. Only a new amendment would guarantee suffrage to all American women.

form a new group, the National Woman Suffrage Association (NWSA). Susan B. Anthony also played a key role in the new group, which decided it would not admit men. The NWSA wanted to address women's suffrage through a constitutional amendment. The group also dealt with labor issues for both men and women and with divorce laws, which were still a key issue for Stanton. Women reformers who opposed Stanton and Anthony's stance soon formed their own group, the American Woman Suffrage Association (AWSA). The AWSA wanted to take a less radical approach and focus on winning suffrage state by state. The group rejected such issues as labor reform and divorce laws, and it allowed men to join.

Also in 1869, Stanton made her first lecture tour. For months at a time, she traveled across the United States, speaking on women's rights and suffrage. During this era, many speakers made similar tours.

The lectures gave people a chance to get out of their houses, meet other people, and learn about new subjects. The lectures were also a form of entertainment. At this time, television, radio, recorded music, and films did not exist.

Stanton made these lecture tours for 12 years. In her autobiography, she described the low points of her constant travel. They included "long journeys" on "overheated … [railroad] cars," "babies crying in our audiences," and "the rain … leaking on the platform." But for Stanton, the problems were worth

An 1869 political cartoon shows what many felt about women in the suffrage movement.

the effort. With her lectures, she educated many people at once about women's rights. And when she was not on stage, she met with small groups of local women. Stanton talked to them about issues such as marriage and women's health.

During her travels, Stanton visited Utah. In 1870, when Utah was still a territory—before it became a U.S. state—its government gave women the right to vote. Stanton visited Utah shortly after this happened. Women in Utah kept their right to vote when the territory became a state in 1896. During Stanton's lifetime, several other Western states and territories gave women the right to vote. She kept fighting to make sure all American women enjoyed that right.

In 1869, Wyoming became the first U.S. state or territory to grant women suffrage. Women in Utah, however, actually voted first, because that territory held local elections in 1870 just after giving women the vote. The first elections held in Wyoming that included women came a little later in the year. Wyoming, like Utah, kept women's suffrage when the territory became a state in 1890.

Stanton made her trip to Utah with Susan B. Anthony. She always called Anthony her best friend. Together, they were the strength of the women's movement for decades. Yet during the early 1870s, Stanton did not always treat Anthony as a true friend. In 1870, they sold *The Revolution*. The newspaper had lost money, and Stanton refused to help Anthony pay the debt. Stanton also did not always defend her friend when newspapers attacked her views. Stanton used humor to win over crowds, but Anthony was usually more serious and direct. The two women might say the same things, but crowds would find

Stanton and Anthony communicated their message of women's rights in different ways.

Anthony's words harsher, leading the newspapers to criticize her.

Stanton traveled while her children were at school. The money she made on the tours helped pay for her sons' college education. During the summer, she stayed with her children at a home the Stantons had bought in Tenafly, New Jersey. Henry still spent most of his time in New York City, where he once again worked as a lawyer.

Stanton also still found time to write. She wrote out the talks she gave on her lecture tours. One of these talks she called "Home Life." The speech focused on marriage and divorce. She said men were not willing to accept women as equals in politics because they were not ready to recognize it in the home. She called for giving women the same rights as men in marriage and divorce.

In 1876, the United States celebrated the 100th anniversary of the Declaration of Independence. To mark the occasion, Anthony asked Stanton to write another declaration of rights for women. At first, Stanton was not eager to help. At 61 years old, Stanton had become overweight and her health was not always strong. She also believed younger women should start taking over the suffrage movement. But in the end, she helped write the document. Stanton and Anthony were joined by Lucretia Mott and Matilda Joslyn Gage. Anthony and

Stanton had known Gage since the 1850s. The women struck an angry tone in their declaration:

> *We protest against this government of the United States as … not a true republic; and we protest against this … celebration of the independence of the United States.*

As they prepared the new declaration of rights, Stanton, Anthony, and Gage began work on a new project. They wanted to write a history of the women's suffrage movement. At first, they expected to produce just a short book. Instead, they worked for more than 10 years and wrote three massive volumes called *History of Woman Suffrage.* Stanton and Anthony did most of the work. They often sat around a large desk at the Stanton home, surrounded by documents, pens, and pencils. The two women sometimes quarreled as they worked. Stanton's daughter Margaret later recalled these arguments. At times she thought the long friendship between the

The first volume of History of Woman Suffrage appeared in 1881 and the second in 1882. The last of the three volumes that Stanton worked on was published in 1887. In the book, Stanton, Anthony, and Gage included letters, news-paper articles, and speeches that outlined the decades-long fight for women's political rights. Three more volumes were written, but Stanton did not work on them. In all, the six volumes of History of Woman Suffrage contain almost 6,000 pages.

two suffragists was about to end. Instead, she would soon see her mother and Anthony "walking down the hill, arm in arm," and then return to work, "as if nothing had ever happened."

The four years spent working on that first book were busy, happy ones for Stanton. In addition to that project, she still gave lectures, and her children were graduating from college and getting married. Stanton also found time for dinner parties, dances, and picnics with her friends and neighbors in Tenafly. She also took on greater duties in the NWSA.

In 1877, Anthony stepped down as president of the NWSA so Stanton could take over. Anthony remained the main organizer for the group, while Stanton served as its public leader. With her small, round body and her curly hair turned completely white, Stanton looked like a loving grandmother. But as one reporter noted, her words were still like "bayonet thrusts ... and gun shots."

As always, Stanton was eager for a constitutional amendment for women's suffrage. In 1878, she convinced California Senator Arlen Sargent to propose a suffrage amendment. The amendment read, "The rights of citizens to vote shall not be denied or abridged by the United States or by any State on account of sex." Stanton also traveled to Washington, D.C., to speak about women's rights.

She was angered by the U.S. senators who ignored her while she spoke. And she had to listen to lawmakers who shared the view of one senator who said the "proper sphere of woman is the family circle, as wife and mother, and not as politician and voter." Still, the women's movement had a friend in Senator Sargent, and over the next few decades more men would support universal suffrage. 🐚

Stanton spoke at meetings of the NWSA throughout the 1870s.

8 REFORMER TO THE END

❧✦❧

While working on *History of Woman Suffrage*, Elizabeth Cady Stanton also found time to travel. In 1882, she sailed to France with her daughter Harriot. Like her mother, Harriot Stanton was a devoted suffragist. On the trip, Stanton visited her son Theodore. He had studied in France, and after marrying a French woman, he settled there. Theodore and his wife gave Stanton her first grandchild, a girl named for her. Stanton's trip, however, was hardly a vacation. As always, she had the energy to discuss the women's movement, and she met with French reformers. She also helped Theodore write a book about women's rights in Europe.

From France, Stanton traveled to Great Britain.

Elizabeth Cady Stanton and Susan B. Anthony continued their friendship and working relationship all their lives.

Harriot Stanton also became a leader of the women's movement. In 1882, she married William Blatch, an Englishman, and became active in the British suffragist movement. In 1902, Harriot Stanton Blatch moved to New York, and she led the efforts to win women's suffrage in her home state. She organized the first large suffrage parade, to draw attention to the women's demands. About 10,000 women marched through the streets of New York City holding banners and signs calling for women's suffrage.

She was pleased to attend a ceremony celebrating suffrage for women in local elections in Glasgow, Scotland. There she made her first speech ever in Europe. About 5,000 people crowded into a church for the occasion. Stanton noted how they gave her and the other speakers "the wildest applause; the entire audience rising, waving their handkerchiefs, and clapping their hands."

Stanton spent about a year in Great Britain. She attended meetings on women's rights and met with well-known British reformers. She also spent time with Susan B. Anthony, who was also visiting Europe. The two women returned to the United States together at the end of 1883.

During the 1880s, Stanton became more interested in the effect of organized religion on women. She was convinced that the teachings of Christianity had prevented women from achieving equality. At the 1885 convention of the NWSA, she strongly supported a resolution that said "male and female [were] ... given equal rights over the earth, but none over each other." Stanton said the teachings of all major religions denied women their rights. But since most Americans were Christians, she focused on the dangers of that faith for women. These ideas were not popular, especially among people who accepted the traditional Christian view that men were superior to women.

In November 1885, Stanton's suffragist friends celebrated her 70th birthday. Henry Stanton turned 80 that year, and his friends gave him a party as well. Although Elizabeth was still active, old age and illness were beginning to slow down her husband. For a time in 1886, he was very sick, but he recovered, and Elizabeth decided to make another trip to Europe. In January 1887, while on that trip, she received sad news: Henry had died of pneumonia, a disease of the lungs.

The Stantons had spent more time together in the years just before Henry's death. Still, some relatives said the two had not been close during their last years. Elizabeth did not leave Europe to attend Henry's funeral. In her autobiography, Stanton described her activities in Europe during that trip, but she did not mention Henry's death. One historian claims that Elizabeth did not love Henry, although they were always good friends.

Stanton remained in Europe until March 1888, once again spending time with reformers and reading the works of great writers. When she returned, she prepared for the first International Council of Women. The NWSA held this event during its annual meeting in Washington, D.C. Stanton described the progress women had made since the Seneca Falls convention of 1848. Women were more active in politics, even though most still could not vote. They had the right to own property and attend colleges. But suffrage was still the true goal, and it would help everyone, not just women. "When woman's voice is heard in government," she told the convention, "our legislation will become more

The Executive Committee of the International Council of Women posed for this photo in 1888.

humane and judgments in our courts be tempered with mercy."

In the years after the International Council, Stanton saw a gap growing between her and Susan B. Anthony. Although the two remained good friends, they had different ideas about the women's movement. As Stanton wrote in her diary, "I get more radical as I get older, while [Anthony] seems to grow more conservative." Anthony wanted to focus solely on suffrage, and she was willing to work with the less-radical American Woman Suffrage Association. She also became friendly with members of the Women's Christian Temperance Union, which also supported suffrage. Stanton had no use for the Christian views of that group.

In 1890, the NWSA and the AWSA united to form the National American Woman Suffrage Association (NAWSA). For the first time since 1869, all the leading American suffragists were working together for a common goal. Stanton worried that the new group would forget other issues that were important to her, such as marriage, divorce, and women's health. Still, she accepted the presidency of the NAWSA. Anthony had also been a candidate for the job, but she asked members to vote for Stanton.

After winning the election, Stanton returned to Europe, leaving Anthony in charge of the new organization. Once again, Stanton remained overseas for

Elizabeth Cady Stanton with her daugher Harriot Stanton Blatch and granddaughter Nora

about 18 months. During that time, she visited with her children and the growing number of grandchildren they added to the family.

By 1891, Stanton noted to a friend, her weight had ballooned to 240 pounds (108 kilograms). She was often short of breath. She also needed help walking, and over the next few years her eyesight began to fail. Stanton's physical problems worsened after two falls. After the second one, she walked using two canes. Yet her mind was as sharp as ever, and she remained angry about the treatment of women in the United States.

In January 1892, Stanton stepped down as president of the NAWSA. She gave a farewell speech that she called "The Solitude of Self." Stanton believed this speech to be the best thing she had ever written, and she thought her audience liked it as well. Susan B. Anthony, however, did not like the speech so much—at least not at first. She thought that Stanton was straying too far from the issue of suffrage. Later, though, Anthony called "The Solitude of Self" "the strongest … argument and appeal ever made … for the full freedom and franchise of women."

In her farewell speech, Stanton argued that each individual woman was ultimately responsible for her own life. Men also faced this "solitude of self," but they did not have to confront laws and attitudes that limited their actions. A woman needed to be able to rely on herself. That meant women needed every chance to educate themselves and find the jobs that best suited their talents. Women needed legal rights that let them be in charge of their lives, since men could not live their lives for them.

Stanton also continued to work on a project she had started years before. With a group of other women, she had been studying the Bible to see exactly what it had to say about women and their roles. Those studies led to *The Woman's Bible*, which was published in 1895. Stanton hated the idea that Christians believed women had brought evil into the world. This notion came from the story of Adam and Eve, in which Eve, the first woman, disobeyed God and ate fruit God had said she could not have. Ever since then, women have been blamed for committing the first sin and angering God. Using historical documents, Stanton and the other authors of *The Woman's Bible* tried to explain how the people who wrote the Bible created a harsh and unfair image of women.

Stanton believed the Bible's treatment of Eve influenced society's views on women.

The Woman's Bible sparked outrage. Stanton claimed that God did not directly give humans the teachings found in the Bible, as many Christians believed. She also upset men who thought women had no right to offer a view on the Bible—especially if it did not agree with what church leaders taught. Stanton, however, said women had to question those leaders, since all of them were men.

Stanton's religious beliefs had changed a great deal from her early life during the Second Great Awakening. In her personal life, Stanton had stopped going to church. She saw God as a being who was both male and female. Her ideas shocked most Americans. They accepted traditional beliefs about God, which saw God as a male, the "Father" of all humans. Even most members of the NAWSA opposed Stanton's book. They saw that her ideas upset many people, and they did not want to lose support for women's suffrage.

The uproar over *The Woman's Bible* forced Stanton to the fringes of the women's movement. She would no longer play a major role in the fight for suffrage. The younger women taking over the NAWSA now looked to Susan B. Anthony for guidance instead of Stanton. In a letter written in 1901, Stanton complained that the new suffragists gave Anthony "thousands of dollars, jewels, laces, silks and satins." All they had given her was "criticisms … for my radical ideas."

But in 1895, before *The Woman's Bible* first appeared, Stanton was still a beloved leader of the movement. In November 1895, Anthony organized a surprise 80th birthday party for her longtime friend. Stanton later wrote that she was more used to blame than praise and was deeply moved by the love and respect her friends showed her at the party.

In the last years of her life, Stanton spent most of her time in an apartment in New York City. She continued to write many articles and letters. She also published her autobiography, *Eighty Years and More*, in 1898. In 1901, she wrote in her diary, "I am always busy, which is perhaps the chief reason why I am always well." From time to time, Anthony asked Stanton to write speeches for her. When she was not writing, Stanton read and took naps.

In June 1902, Anthony visited Stanton at her apartment. The two made plans to see each other again that November, on Stanton's 87th birthday. In the months that followed, Stanton wrote several letters. Two of them were to President Theodore Roosevelt and his wife, asking them to support the suffrage amendment. They were the last letters Stanton ever wrote. On October 26, she died at home of heart failure.

Elizabeth Cady Stanton did not live to see women win the right to vote. That right would not come until 1920, after Congress had passed what became the 19th Amendment and the states had ratified it. But Stanton had helped turn the women's movement into a powerful force for women's rights.

With those efforts, Stanton made enemies. She sometimes spoke harshly against people who did not support the ideals she held so strongly. But her ideas and energy helped set women on the path to equality, in the United States and around the world. ✑

To many, Stanton and Anthony are as important to the cause of liberty as George Washington.

STANTON'S LIFE

1833
Graduates from Troy
Female Seminary;
returns to Johnstown

1815
Born on November 12
in Johnstown,
New York

1830
Graduates from the
Johnstown Academy

1815

1826
The first photograph
is taken by Joseph
Niépce, a French
physicist

1833
Great Britain
abolishes slavery

WORLD EVENTS

1840

Marries Henry
Stanton on May 1;
attends World Anti-
Slavery Convention
in England

1848

Helps organize the
first convention for
women's rights and
writes the Declaration
of Sentiments,
which calls for
women's suffrage

1840

1846

Irish potato famine
reaches its worst

1848

*The Communist
Manifesto*, by
German writers Karl
Marx and Friedrich
Engels, is widely
distributed

STANTON'S LIFE

1851

Meets Susan B. Anthony, beginning a long friendship and partnership to win women's rights

1854

Speaks to the New York State Legislature, calling for equal rights for women

1863

Founds the Women's Loyal National League, to support the Civil War and the effort to free all U.S. slaves

1860

1852

Postage stamps are widely used

1865

Lewis Carroll writes *Alice's Adventures in Wonderland*

WORLD EVENTS

1868

Serves as editor of a suffragist newspaper called *The Revolution*

1869

Forms the National Woman Suffrage Association (NWSA); begins first lecture tour across the United States

1876

Begins writing *History of Woman Suffrage*

1870

1869

The periodic table of elements is invented by Dimitri Mendeleyev

1892

Writes one of her
most famous speeches,
"The Solitude of Self"

1890

Becomes president of
the newly created
National American
Woman Suffrage
Association

1890

1893

Women gain voting
privileges in New
Zealand, the first
country to take such
a step

WORLD EVENTS

1895

Publishes *The Woman's Bible*, angering many by challenging traditional ideas about women and religion

1898

Publishes her autobiography, *Eighty Years and More*

1902

Dies on October 26 in New York City

1900

1896

The Olympic Games are held for the first time in recent history in Athens, Greece

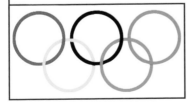

1901

First exhibition of Pablo Picasso opens

DATE OF BIRTH: November 12, 1815

PLACE OF BIRTH: Johnstown, New York

FATHER: Daniel Cady (1773–1859)

MOTHER: Margaret Livingston Cady (1785–1871)

SPOUSE: Henry Brewster Stanton (1805–1887)

DATE OF MARRIAGE: May 1, 1840

CHILDREN: Daniel Cady Stanton ("Neil") (1842–1891)

Henry Brewster Stanton Jr. ("Kit") (1844–1903)

Gerrit Smith Stanton ("Gat") (1845–1927)

Theodore Weld Stanton ("Theo") (1851–1925)

Margaret Livingston Stanton (1852–1938?)

Harriot Eaton Stanton (1856–1940)

Robert Livingston Stanton (1859–1920)

DATE OF DEATH: October 26, 1902

PLACE OF BURIAL: Woodlawn Cemetery, New York City